God Bless America
Journal

Edited and Compiled by
Paul C. Brownlow

Dedicated to the victims and families of the
September 11, 2001, tragedy.

Ten percent of the proceeds of this book are
being donated to The American Red Cross to
support the families of those who lost their lives
in our national tragedy.

Copyright © 2001 Brownlow Corporation
6309 Airport Freeway
Fort Worth, Texas 76117

Compiled by Paul C. Brownlow

All rights reserved. No part of this book may be
reproduced in any form without permission in writing
from the publisher.

References taken from Holy Bible, New International
Version (NIV) copyright © 1973, 1978, 1984 by
International Bible Society. Used by permission.

ISBN 1-57051-034-2

Printed in the United States of America

This is a blank book. It may be used for anything, but it has been especially designed for those wanting to chronicle their emotions and prayers as they live through the events of our time.

The thought-provoking quotations remind us of our country's dependence on God, as well as our personal need for Him.

Journaling has become more popular in recent years, but it has always been of great value. The process of sorting out our feelings and putting them into words and recording them is extremely helpful and therapeutic. Research studies continue to prove that journaling promotes and quickens the healing process—both emotionally and physically. And when our hearts are turned toward God, the spiritual blessings are innumerable.

May God Bless America.

O beautiful for spacious skies,
For amber waves of grain,
For purple mountain majesties
Above the fruited plain!
America! America!
God shed His grace on thee
And crown thy good with brotherhood
From sea to shining sea!

I am sure that never was a people, who had more reason to acknowledge a Divine interposition in their affairs, than those of the United States.
—President George Washington

Hear my prayer, O God; listen to the words of my mouth. Strangers are attacking me; ruthless men seek my life—men without regard for God. Surely God is my help; the LORD is the one who sustains me.
—Psalm 54:2–4

> This generation of Americans has a
> rendezvous with destiny.
> —President Franklin D. Roosevelt

There are times when God asks nothing of his children except silence, patience, and tears.
—Charles Seymour Robinson

Reflect upon your present blessings of which
every man has many; not on your past misfortunes
of which all men have some.
—Charles Dickens

**God grants liberty only to those who love it,
and are always ready to guard it.**
—Daniel Webster

America is great because America is good, and if America ever ceases to be good, America will cease to be great.
—Alexis de Tocqueville
(19th Century French writer and statesman)

Our Lord, our God, deliver us from the fear of what might happen and give us the grace to enjoy what now is and to keep striving after what out to be.
—Peter Marshall

The LORD is close to the brokenhearted
and saves those who are crushed in spirit.
A righteous man may have many troubles,
but the LORD delivers him from them all.
—Psalm 34:18–19

We must not only affirm the brotherhood of man; we must live it.
—Henry Codman Potter

Learn to keep the sacred things of life sacred.
—Paul C. Brownlow

The God who gave us life, gave us liberty at the same time.
—President Thomas Jefferson

Patriotism consists not in waving the flag,
but in striving that our country shall be
righteous as well as strong.
—James Bryce

I walk with God daily.
—Helen Keller

If my people, who are called by my name, will humble themselves and pray and seek my face and turn from their wicked ways, then will I hear from heaven and will forgive their sin and will heal their land.

—2 Chronicles 7:14

> Even if I knew certainly the world would end tomorrow, I would plant an apple tree today.
> —Martin Luther

Evil may have its hour, but God will have His day.
−Bishop Fulton Sheen

There is not enough darkness in all the world to put out the light of one small candle.

—Anonymous

If we are not governed by God,
then we will be ruled by tyrants.
—William Penn

Teach me your way, O LORD; lead me in a straight path because of my oppressors. Do not turn me over to the desire of my foes,…breathing out violence. I am still confident of this: I will see the goodness of the LORD in the land of the living. Wait for the LORD; be strong and take heart and wait for the LORD.
—Psalm 27:11–14

We on this continent should never forget that men first crossed the Atlantic not to find soil for their ploughs but to secure liberty for their souls.
—Robert J. McCracken

I have lived to thank God that all of my prayers have not been answered.
—Jean Ingelow

**The man who has not tasted the bitter
does not know what the sweet is.**
—Jewish Proverb

Those who expect to reap the blessings of freedom
must, like men, undergo the fatigue of supporting it.
—Thomas Paine

Come unto me all you who are weary and
heavy-ladened, and I will give you rest.
—Matthew 11:28

It is not because things are good that we are to thank the Lord, but because He is good.
—Hannah Whitall Smith

Oh, say, can you see, by the dawn's early light, What so proudly we hailed at the twilight's last gleaming, Whose broad stripes and bright stars through the perilous fight, O'er the ramparts we watched were so gallantly streaming? And the rockets' red glare, the bombs bursting in air, Gave proof thro' the night that our flag was still there. Oh, say, does that star-spangled banner yet wave O'er the land of the free, and the home of the brave!

–Francis Scott Key

Free at last! Free at last! Thank God Almighty, we are free at last!

—Martin Luther King, Jr.
(Lincoln Memorial Speech, 1963)

Learn to hold loosely all that is not eternal.
—Agnes Maud Rayden

> Those who deny freedom to others deserve it not for themselves, and, under a just God, cannot long retain it.
> —President Abraham Lincoln

My soul finds rest in God alone; my salvation comes from him. He alone is my rock and my salvation; he is my fortress, I will never be shaken.
—Psalm 62:1–2

> I am certain that, however great the hardships and the trials which loom ahead, our America will endure and the cause of human freedom will triumph.
> —Cordell Hunt

I would rather work with God in the dark
than go alone in the light.
—Mary Gardiner Brainard

Those who have a "why" to live, can bear with almost any "how".
−Victor Frankel

Territory is but the body of a nation. The people who inhabit its hills and valleys are its soul, its spirit, its life.
—President James A. Garfield

> God is our refuge and strength, an ever-present help in trouble. Therefore we will not fear, though the earth give way and the mountains fall into the sea.
> —Psalm 46:1–2

No people on earth have more cause to be thankful than ours, and this is said reverently, in no spirit of boastfulness in our own strength, but with the gratitude to the Giver of good who has blessed us.
—President Theodore Roosevelt

God will not look you over for medals,
degrees, or diplomas, but for scars.
—Elbert G. Hubbard

Freedom and duty always go hand in hand and if the free do not accept the duty of social responsibility, they will not long remain free.
—John Foster Dulles

> To live through a period of stress and sorrow with another human being creates a bond which nothing seems able to break.
> —Eleanor Roosevelt

Exalted be God my Savior! He is the God who
subdues nations, who saves me from my enemies.
—Psalm 18:47–48

Whether God blesses America or not does not depend so much upon God as it does upon us Americans.
—C. H. Kopf

Jesus did not come to explain away suffering or
remove it. He came to fill it with his presence.
—Paul Claudel

The world is now too dangerous for anything but the truth, too small for anything but brotherhood.
–Adlai Stevenson

America was founded by people who believe that God was their rock of safety. I recognize we must be cautious in claiming that God is on our side, but I think it's all right to keep asking if we're on His side.
—President Ronald Reagan

Therefore we do not lose heart. Though outwardly we are wasting away, yet inwardly we are being renewed day by day. For our light and momentary troubles are achieving for us an eternal glory that far outweighs them all. So we fix our eyes not on what is seen, but on what is unseen. For what is seen is temporary, but what is unseen is eternal.
—2 Corinthians 4:16–18

God has laid upon us the duty of being free, of safeguarding freedom of spirit, no matter how difficult that may be, or how much sacrifice and suffering it may require.
—Nicholai Berdyaev

All great things are simple, and many can be expressed in single words: freedom, justice, honor, duty, mercy, hope.
—Sir Winston Churchill

God takes life's pieces and gives us unbroken peace.
−W. D. Gough

We have been the recipients of the choicest bounties of Heaven. We have been preserved these many years in peace and prosperity. We have grown in numbers, wealth, and power as no other nation has ever grown. But we have forgotten God.
—President Abraham Lincoln

The plans of the LORD stand firm forever,
the purposes of his heart through all generations.
Blessed is the nation whose God is the LORD.
—Psalm 33:11–12

> It is by no means necessary that a great nation should always stand at the heroic level. But no nation has the root of greatness in it unless in time of need it can rise to the heroic level.
> —President Theodore Roosevelt

**If you would have God hear you when you pray,
you must hear Him when He speaks.**
–Thomas Benton Brooks

> After what I owe to God, nothing should be more dear or sacred to me than the love and respect I owe to my country.
> —Jacques Auguste de Thou

Righteousness exalts a nation.
—Proverbs 14:34

The capacity to care gives life its deepest significance.
—Pablo Casals

But all of us—at home, at war, wherever we may be—are within the reach of God's love and power. We all can pray. We all should pray. We should ask the fulfillment of God's will.
—President Harry S. Truman

**When life knocks you to your knees,
you're in a position to pray.**

Courage for the great sorrows of life, and patience for the small ones, and when you have laboriously accomplished your daily task, go to sleep in peace. God is awake.
—Victor Hugo

> Be still, and know that I am God;
> I will be exalted among the nations,
> I will be exalted in the earth.
> —Psalm 46:10

I used to pray that God would do this or that. Now I pray God will make His will known to me.
—Mme. Chiang Kai-Shek

And so, my fellow Americans—ask not what your country can do for you—ask what you can do for your country. Let us go forth to lead the land we love, asking His blessing and His help, but knowing that here on earth God's work must truly be our own.

—President John F. Kennedy